The Chronology

of the

Gospel of Jesus Christ

Denis R. Manley

ISBN: 978-1-78364-527-5

www.obt.org.uk

****

The Open Bible
Fordland Mount, Upper Basildon,
Reading, RG8 8LU, UK.

The Chronology of the Gospel of Jesus Christ

Contents

Page

PREFACE

PREFACE

We have four records of the life and teaching of Jesus Christ, to which has been appended (sometime after they were written) the word ‘Gospel’. Hence we have “The Gospel according to St. Matthew... St. Mark... etc.” And these four, and these four only, form part of the Bible.

These four were evidently written from different perspectives – each Evangelist looking at Jesus Christ from his own point of view. In this booklet those perspectives are presented as seeing the Lord Jesus Christ as King (Matthew), Servant (Mark), Man (Luke) and God (John).

However, there have been many attempts over the centuries to harmonise these four accounts. Probably the earliest was that of Titian, who became a disciple of Justin Martyr (circa 160). His chief claim to fame is his work Diatessaron (i.e. one gospel from four).

Modern man likes biographies and events presented in chronological order, whereas the ancient eastern mind often grouped similar or contrasting ideas. Thus by reading down the ‘Events’ column of the charts on subsequent pages, the reader will rapidly gain an appreciation not only of what Christ did, but also the order in which He did those things. The Scripture references from the relevant Gospels are clearly displayed and can be referred to should further information be wanted.

Some see Luke as having written his account chronologically, because of his use of the expression “orderly account” (Luke 1:3).

However, I favour Matthew as being more chronological, and have used his Gospel as my yard-stick.

With that in mind, this book sets forth in chronological order a harmonized account of the Four Gospel records, with a summary of each Gospel. It shows that each of the four writers had a distinctive message for a particular group of people, yet their writings harmonise wonderfully, which should not surprise us for "Holy men of God spoke as they were moved by the Holy Spirit" (2 Peter 1:21; NKJV).

Denis Manley

SUMMARY OF THE GOSPEL OF MATTHEW

SUMMARY OF THE GOSPEL OF MATTHEW

INTRODUCTION

1. Written by the Apostle Matthew, ex-tax collector 9:9.

2. Written to Jews in Aramaic, the language of the Jews at that time.

3. Written c.35 A.D., occasioned by the persecution and scattering of the Jews at Jerusalem. Acts 8:1-4.
Excludes The Day of Grace, as does the Old Testament.

SUBJECT

1. ‘’Behold your King.’ Zech. 9:9.

2. ‘A branch of righteousness, a King.’ Jer. 23:5.

3. ‘The lion of the tribe of Judah.’ Rev. 4:7; 5:5.

4. 'The Day of the Lord - that day.' Matt. 7:22; 24:36
'The Lord alone will be exalted in that day.' Isa. 2:12-17.

OUTLINE

1. The King's credentials. Ch. 1 to 4:16.
   The witness of the scriptures to Christ.
   Keynote: 'Born King of the Jews'. 2:2.

2. The King's witness to the nation's rulers. 4:17- to 11:24.
   Keynote: The requirements of the Kingdom. Ch. 5-7.

3. The King's witness to his subjects. 11:25 to 16:20.
   Keynote: The parables of the Kingdom. Ch. 13.

4. The King's witness to his Apostles. 16:21 to 25:46.
   Keynote: The coming of the Kingdom. Ch. 24 & 25.

5. The death and resurrection of the King. Ch. 26 to 28.
   Keynote: 'The King of the Jews'. 27:37.

Note the opening verse of each section

CHRONOLOGY

It is the conviction of this writer that the events recorded by Matthew are in chronological order except for 21:18-19. Written shortly after the events by an eye-witness for the most part, with the co-operation of the other apostles at Jerusalem, under the direction of the Holy Spirit. 'The scriptures of the (NT) prophets.' Rom 16:26.

SUMMARY OF THE GOSPEL OF MARK

SUMMARY OF THE GOSPEL OF MARK

INTRODUCTION

1. Written by John Mark, an associate of Peter (Acts 12:12) and Paul (Acts 12:25).

2. Written to Romans in Greek, incorporating Latin words and explains Jewish phrases and customs.

3. Probably written c.52-54 A.D. when Mark returned to his home at Jerusalem (Acts 12:12), after accompanying his uncle Barnabas (Col. 4:10; AV) to Cyprus (Acts 15:39).

4. Excludes the birth and early life of Jesus. A servant's pedigree is unimportant, but his obedience is all-important. Note the words 'Straightway' and 'Immediately' which occur frequently.

SUBJECT

1. 'Behold my servant'. Isa. 42:1.

2. 'My servant the branch'. Zech. 3:8.

3. The lowly ox-calf. Rev. 4:7. (Cf. Matt 11:29).

4. 'I delight to do your will O my God'. Ps. 40:8 (Cf. Mark 10:45).

OUTLINE

1. The servant SON. 1:1-13.

2. The servant at work in Galilee. 1:14 to 9:50.

3. The servant goes to Jerusalem. Ch. 10 to 13.

4. The servant obedient unto death. Ch. 14 & 15.

5. The servant exalted. Ch. 16 (Cf. Phil. 2:5-11).

CHRONOLOGY

In chronological order except for the following:-

3:13-19. This event must have occurred earlier than in Mark's account as it is relevant to 6:7-13, see below.

4:3-5 to 5:43 & 6:7-13. These events are placed by Mark after the parables of the kingdom. They actually occurred after the Sermon on the Mount as Matthew makes clear. The Sermon on the Mount is not included by Mark, which explains why the events in question are placed out of sequence.

SUMMARY OF THE GOSPEL OF LUKE

SUMMARY OF THE GOSPEL OF LUKE

INTRODUCTION

1. Written by Luke, the physician (Col. 4:14), and companion of the apostle Paul (Acts 16:10).

2. Written to Theophilus, a Greek (1:3). Possibly a personal acquaintance of Luke.

3. Probably written c.58-60 A.D. during Paul's imprisonment at Caesarea. (Acts ch. 23 & 24).

4. Contains much material which is exclusive to Luke.

SUBJECT

1. 'Behold the man whose name is the Branch'. Zech. 6:12

2. The (perfect) man. Rev. 4:7

3. The Son of man from heaven. John 3:13

4. The second Adam. 1 Co 15:45. Luke 19:10

OUTLINE

1. The early life of Jesus. 1:1 to 4:13.

2. 'All that Jesus began to do'. 4:14 to 10:24 (Acts 1:1).

3. 'All that Jesus began to teach'. 10:25 to 21:38 (Acts 1:1).

4. The death and resurrection of Jesus. 22:1 to 24:53.

CHRONOLOGY

The gospel of Luke is often taken as being in chronological order because he says, 'I write unto thee in order' 1:3 (AV). This is better translated as, 'An orderly account (NKJV), or 'With method' (JND).

The method is an arrangement of firstly 'miracles' and then 'Teaching'. As Luke puts it in Acts 1:1, 'All that Jesus began to do and to teach.' See the outline above.

In the section on miracles Luke closely follows Mark's account. The section on teaching (which was probably often repeated) contains much material which is exclusive to Luke. This cannot be placed chronologically and is therefore listed separately at the end of this booklet.

SUMMARY OF THE GOSPEL OF JOHN

SUMMARY OF THE GOSPEL OF JOHN

INTRODUCTION

1. Written by the apostle John 21:24. The disciple whom Jesus loved. 13:23.

2. Written for the Jewish Dispersion. 20:30-31.

3. Traditionally believed to have been written c.85-89 A.D. from Ephesus, shortly before John was banished to the isle of Patmos.

4. The events recorded occur mainly in Jerusalem rather than Galilee as in the other gospel accounts, from which this one is distinct.

SUBJECT

1. 'Behold your God'. Isa. 40:9.

2. 'The Branch of the Lord'. Isa. 4:2 (Cf. Isa. 11:1).

3. The flying eagle. Rev. 4:7.

4. The **Son of God**. John 3:16.

OUTLINE

1. 'The **WORD** became flesh', 'the Lamb of God'. Ch. 1.

2. His public ministry. Ch. 2 to 12.

3. His ministry to his own. Ch. 13 to 17.

4. The (Passover) Lamb slain. Ch. 18 & 19. (1 Co. 5:7).

5. The Lord in resurrection power. Ch. 20 & 21.

CHRONOLOGY

In harmony with Matthew's account and in chronological order except for the following:-

12:2-11. The anointing at Bethany. Note v. 2 simply says, 'There they made him a supper', without any reference to time. It is the conviction of this writer that Jesus had a supper each evening at Bethany, when he went out to the Mount of Olives (Luke 21:37-38). This would include the Sunday, Monday and Tuesday, as well as the day of his arrival (John 12:1).

Both Matthew and Mark make it clear that the anointing took place on the Tuesday evening. The events of Monday and Tuesday are omitted by John, which explains why the anointing appears out of place.

SUMMARY OF THE FINAL DAYS AT JERUSALEM

SUMMARY OF THE FINAL DAYS AT JERUSALEM

GENTILE DAYS	JEWISH DAYS	TIME	EVENTS	REF.
Friday	8th. Nisan (Abib)	12:00	Jesus come to **Bethany**, six days	Jn 12:1
		18:00	before	
		00:00	Passover	
	9th. Nisan	06:00	Weekly Sabbath rest	
Saturday		12:00		
		18:00		
		00:00		
	10th.Nisan	06:00	**THE LAMB PROVED FOUR DAYS (**Ex 12:3-6)	
Sunday		12:00	The King welcomed at Jerusalem Mt 21:1-11	
		18:00	Goes out to Bethany Mk 11:11	
		00:00		
	11th.Nisan	06:00	The fig tree cursed Mk 11:12-14	
Monday		12:00	Cleanses the **temple** and teaches Mk 11:15-18	
		18:00	Goes out to **Bethany** Mk 11:19	
		00:00		
	12th.Nisan	06:00	The fig tree withered away Mk 11:20-26	
Tuesday		12:00	Teaches in the **temple** Mk 11:27/12:44	
		18:00	Goes out to **the Mount of Olives** Mk 13:1-3	

		00:00	The anointing at **Bethany** Mk 14:1-9
	13th.Nisan	06:00	
Wednesday		12:00	Teaches in the **temple** Jn 12:20-50
		18:00	The Passover supper Mk 14:16-18
		00:00	Goes out to **Gethsemane** Mk 14:26
	14th.Nisan	06:00	**THE LORD'S PASSOVER** (Lev 23:5)
		09:00	Jesus Crucified (1 Co 5:7) Mk 15:21-32
Thursday		12:00	Darkness for three hours Mk 15:33
		15:00	Jesus lays down his life (Jn 10:17-18) Mk 15:34-41
		18:00	The Burial Mk 15:42-47
		00:00	
	15th.Nisan	06:00	**FEAST OF UNLEAVENED BREAD** (Lev 23:6-8)
Friday		12:00	A high day (Sabbath) Jn 19:31
		18:00	
		00:00	
	16th.Nisan	06:00	Weekly Sabbath rest (Lev 23:3) Mk 16:1
Saturday		12:00	
		18:00	
		00:00	**FEAST OF FIRST FRUITS** (Lev 23:9-14)
	17th.Nisan	06:00	**THE RESURRECTION** (Matt 12:40)
Sunday		12:00	Mt 28:1-8 On the road to Emmaus
		18:00	Lk 24:13-27 Jesus appears in the upper room
		00:00	Jn 20:19
	18th.Nisan	06:00	

DETAILED CHRONOLOGICAL INDEX

DETAILED CHRONOLOGICAL INDEX

EVENTS	MATT	MARK	LUKE	JOHN
PREPARATION				
The eternal Word				1:1-18
Birth of John Baptist foretold			1:1-25	
Birth of Jesus foretold			1:26-38	
Mary visit Elizabeth			1:39-45	
Mary rejoices			1:46-56	
Birth and circumcision of John Baptist			1:57-66	
Zechariah's prophecy			1:67-80	
The genealogy of Jesus	1:1-17		3:23-38	
5 B.C. to 8 A.D.				
The birth of Jesus at Bethlehem	1:18-25		2:1-7	
The Shepherds			2:8-20	
Circumcision of Jesus			2:21	
Jesus presented in the Temple			2:22-38	
The wise men	2:1-12			
The flight into **Egypt**	2:13-15			
Massacre of the innocents	2:16-18			
Return to **Nazareth**	2:19-23		2:39-40	
To **Jerusalem** for Passover			2:41-45	
Jesus in the Temple, twelve years old			2:46-50	

8 A.D. to 26 A.D.

Jesus subject to Mary and Joseph			2:51-52	

26 A.D.

A voice crying in the wilderness	3:1-12	1:1-8	3:1-20	1:19-28
Jesus baptized	3:13-17	1:9-11	3:21-22	
Jesus tempted by Satan	4:1-11	1:12-13	4:1-13	
The Lamb of God				1:29-36
The first disciples				1:37-51

JESUS BEGINS HIS MINISTRY

Goes to **Galilee**	4:12	1:14-15	4:14-15	1:43
First miracle, water turned to wine				2:1-11
Rejected at **Nazareth**			4:16-30	
Goes to **Capernaum**	4:13-17		4:31-32	2:12
Four disciples called	4:18-22	1:16-20	5:1-11	

27 A.D.

Jesus goes to Jerusalem for Passover				2:13
Cleanses the Temple, many believe				2:14-25
Nicodemus and the new birth				3:1-21
Jesus makes disciples in **Judea**				3:22 (4:1-2)
Disciples baptized at **Aenon** (In retrospect. Cf. Jn 1:35-37 & Mt 4:12)				3:23-24
John Baptist testifies to Christ				3:25-36
Returns to **Galilee** through **Samaria**				4:1-4

The woman at Sychar's well				4:5-26
The whitened harvest				4:27-38
The Saviour of the world				4:39-42
Preaching and healing in Galilee	4:23-25	1:21-22		4:43-45
Second miracle, Nobleman's son healed				4:46-54

THE REQUIREMENTS OF THE KINGDOM

(THE SERMON ON THE MOUNT)	Ch. 5-7			
The beatitudes	5:1-2		6:20-26	
Salt and light	5:13-16		14:34-35	
Christ fulfills the law	5:17-20			
Sinful hearts	5:21-30			
Marriage and adultery	5:31-32			
Oaths forbidden	5:33-37			
Go the second mile	5:38-42			
Love your enemies	5:43-48		6:27-36	
Giving that pleases God	6:1-4			
How to pray	6:5-15		11:1-4	
Fasting	6:16-18			
True riches	6:19-24			
Do not worry	6:25-34		12:22, 34	
Do not judge	7:1-6		6:37-42	
Ask, seek, knock	7:7-12		11:9-13	
The narrow way	7:13-14			
False prophets	7:15-20			
I never knew you	7:21-23			
Build on the rock	7:24-29		6:46-49	
Jesus comes down from the mount	8:1			
A leper healed	8:2-4	1:40-45	5:12-16	
Jesus comes to Capernaum	8:5		7:1	
Centurion's servant healed	8:5-13		7:2-10	

Unclean spirit cast out		1:23-28	4:33-37
Peter's mother-in-law healed	8:14-15	1:29-31	4:38-39
Many healed at evening	8:16-17	1:32-34	4:40-41
Preaching and healing in Galilee		1:35-39	4:42-44
Widow of Nain's son raised to life			7:11-17
Jesus goes to Gadera	8:18	4:35	8:22
The cost of discipleship	8:19-22		9:57-62
Jesus stills the waves	8:23-27	4:36-41	8:23-25
Demoniac healed	8:28-34	5:1-21	8:26-39
Jesus returns to Capernaum	9:1	2:1-2	
Paralytic healed	9:2-8	2:3-12	5:17-26
Matthew called	9:9-13	2:13-17	5:27-32
Questioned about fasting	9:14-17	2:18-22	5:33-39
A woman healed	9:18-22	5:22-34	8:40-48
Jairus's daughter raised to life	9:23-26	5:35-43	8:49-56
Two blind men healed	9:27-31		
A demon cast out	9:32-34		
A sinful woman forgiven			7:36-50
Preaching and healing in Galilee	9:35-38		8:1-3
Twelve apostles named	10:1-4	3:13-19	6:12-16
Twelve apostles sent out	10:5-15	6:7-13	9:1-6
Twelve apostles counselled	10:16-42		
Preaching and teaching in Galilee	11:1		
John Baptist sends messengers to Jesus	11:2-19		7:18-35
Seventy others sent out			10:1-12
Woe to the impenitent cities	11:20-24		10:13-16
The seventy return			10:17-20
Jesus rejoices in spirit	11:25-27		10:21-24
Jesus offers true rest	11:28-30		

28 A.D.

Goes to Jerusalem for the Feast (Passover?)				5:1
Man healed at the pool of Bethesda				5:2-15
Honour the Father and the Son				5:16-23
Life and judgment through the Son				5:24-30
The fourfold witness to the Son				5:31-47
The good Samaritan			10:25-37	
The return journey			10:38	
Mary and Martha receive Jesus at Bethany			10:38-42	
Lord of the Sabbath	12:1-8	2:23-28	6:1-5	
Healing on the Sabbath	12:9-14	3:1-6	6:6-11	
By the sea of Galilee		3:7-9		
Jesus heals a great multitude	12:15-16	3:10-12	6:17-19	
'Behold My Servant'	12:17-21			
A house divided cannot stand	12:22-30	3:20-27	11:14-23	
The unpardonable sin	12:31-32	3:28-30		
A tree is known by its fruit	12:33-37		6:43-45	
The sign of Jonah	12:38-42		11:29-32	
The unclean spirit returns	12:43-45		11:24-26	
Jesus's mother and brothers seek him	12:46-50	3:31-35	8:19-21	

THE PARABLES OF THE KINGDOM

Parable of the sower	13:1-9	4:1-9	8:4-8

The purpose of parables	13:10-17	4:10-12	8:9-10	
Parable of the sower explained	13:18-23	4:13-20	8:11-15	
Parable of the wheat and tares	13:24-30			
Parable of the light under a bushel		4:21-25	8:16-18	
Parable of the growing seed		4:26-29		
Parable of the mustard seed	13:31-32	4:30-32	13:18-19	
Parable of the leaven	13:33		13:20-21	
Jesus's use of parables	13:34-35	4:33-34		
Wheat Tares parable explained	13:36-43			
Parable of the hidden treasure	13:44			
Parable of the pearl of great price	13:45-46			
Parable of the dragnet	13:47-52			
Jesus again rejected at Nazareth	13:53-58	6:1-6		
John Baptist beheaded	14:1-12	6:14-29	9:7-9	
The Twelve return and recount their exploits		6:30	9:10	

<u>29 A.D.</u>

Passover, Jesus remains in Galilee				6:4(7:1)
Jesus goes to the desert with the Twelve	14:13	6:31-32	9:10	6:1
Feeding 5000	14:14-21	6:33-44	9:11-17	6:2-14
Jesus walks on the sea	14:22-33	6:45-52		6:15-21

The Bread of Life				6:22-59
Many disciples turn away				6:60-71
Many healed in Gennesaret	14:34-36	6:53-56		
Defilement from within	15:1-20	7:1-23		
A Gentile woman shows her faith	15:21-28	7:24-30		
Deaf and dumb man healed	15:29-31	7:31-37		
Feeding 4000	15:32-39	8:1-10		
Pharisees seek a sign	16:1-4	8:11-12	Cf.12:54-56	
Leaven of the Pharisees and Sadducees	16:5-12	8:13-21		
Blind man healed at **Bethsaida**		8:22-26		
Peter confesses Christ	16:13-20	8:27-30	9:18-20	
Jesus predicts his death and resurrection (1)	16:21-23	8:31-33	9:21-22	
Take up cross and follow him	16:24-28	8:34-9:1	9:23-27	
Jesus transfigured on the mount	17:1-13	9:2-13	9:28-36	
A boy is healed	17:14-21	9:14-29	9:37-42	
Jesus predicts his death and resurrection (2)	17:22-23	9:30-32	9:43-45	
Jesus pays his tax	17:24-27			
'Who is the greatest?'	18:1-5	9:33-37	9:46-48	
Jesus forbids sectarianism		9:38-41	9:49-50	
Jesus warns of offences	18:6-9	9:42-50		
The seeking Saviour	18:10-14			
Dealing with a sinning brother	18:15-20			
Parable of the unforgiving servant	18:21-35			

The Feast of Tabernacles				7:1-9
Jesus goes to Jerusalem for the feast			9:51-56	7:10
Jewish opinions of Jesus				7:11-24
Could this be the Christ?				7:25-31
Jesus and the religious leaders				7:32-36
The promise of the Holy Spirit				7:37-39
Who is Jesus				7:40-44
Jesus rejected by the authorities				7:45-53
Jesus goes to the Mount of Olives				8:1
Jesus returns to the temple				8:2
Adulterous woman brought to Jesus				8:3-11
The Light of the World				8:12-20
Jesus predicts his departure				8:21-29
The truth shall make you free				8:30-36
Abraham's seed and Satan's				8:37-47
Before Abraham was, **I AM**				8:48-59
Man born blind receives sight				9:1-12
Pharisees excommunicate the man				9:13-34
True sight and true blindness				9:35-41
The Door of the Sheep				10:1-10
The Good Shepherd				10:11-21
The Feast of Dedication				10:22-23
The Shepherd knows his sheep				10:24-30
Efforts to stone Jesus				10:31-39
Jesus goes away beyond Jordan	19:1-2	10:1		10:40
Many believe				10:41-42
Marriage and divorce	19:3-10	10:2-12		
Teaching on celibacy	19:11-12			

Little children blessed	19:13-15	10:13-16	18:15-17	
Rich young ruler counselled	19:16-22	10:17-22	18:18-23	
With God all things are possible	19:23-30	10:23-31	18:24-30	
Parable of the workers in the vineyard	20:1-16			
The death of Lazarus				11:1-16
Jesus comes to **Bethany**				11:17
The Resurrection and the Life				11:18-27
Death the last enemy				11:28-37
Lazarus raised to life				11:38-44
The plot to kill Jesus				11:45-57
Goes away to **Ephraim**				11:54
Going up to Jerusalem	20:17	10:32	18:31	
Jesus predicts his death and resurrection (3)	20:18-19	10:32-34	18:31-34	
Greatness is serving	20:20-28	10:35-45		
Enters **Jericho**		10:46	19:1	
Stays at the house of Zacchaeus			19:2-10	
Two blind men given sight	20:29-34	10:46-52	18:35-43	
The parable of the pounds			19:11-28	

30 A.D. THE FINAL DAYS AT JERUSALEM (see summary given earlier.)

FRIDAY

Jesus comes to Bethany				12:1

SUNDAY

King welcomed at Jerusalem	21:1-11	11:1-10	19:29-40	12:12-19
Jesus weeps over Jerusalem			19:41-44	
Enters temple, goes out to Bethany		11:11		

MONDAY

The fig tree cursed	21:18-19	11:12-14	
Jesus cleanses the temple	21:12	11:15-16	19:45-46
Jesus teaches and heals in the temple	21:13-16	11:17-18	19:47-48
Goes out to Bethany	21:17	11:19	

TUESDAY

The fig tree withered away	21:20-22	11:20-26	
Jesus questioned in the temple	21:23-27	11:27-33	20:1-8
Parable of the two sons	21:28-32		
Parable of the wicked vine dressers	21:33-46	12:1-12	20:9-19
Parable of the King's wedding feast	22:1-14		
Pharisees question, 'Paying taxes'	22:15-22	12:13-17	20:20-26
Sadducees question, 'The resurrection'	22:23-33	12:18-27	20:27-40
Scribes question, 'The first commandment'	22:34-40	12:28-34	
Jesus's question, 'How is Christ David's son'	22:41-46	12:35-37	20:41-44

Woe to scribes and Pharisees	23:1-36	12:38-40	20:45-47 Cf.11:37-54	
The widows two mites		12:41-44	21:1-4	
Jesus laments over Jerusalem	23:37-39		13:34-35	
Goes out to the Mount of Olives	24:1-2	13:1-2	21:5-6	

<u>THE COMING OF THE KINGDOM</u>

Signs of the times and the end of the age	24:3-14	13:3-13	21:7-19	
The destruction of Jerusalem			21:20-24	
The great tribulation	24:15-28	13:14-23		
The coming of the Son of Man	24:29-31	13:24-27	21:25-28	
Parable of the fig tree	24:32-35	13:28-31	21:29-33	
Watch therefore...	24:36-44	13:32-37	21:34-38	
The faithful and the evil servants	24:45-51		Cf.12:35-48	
Parable of the wise and foolish virgins	25:1-13			
Parable of the talents	25:14-30			
The Son of Man will judge the nations	25:31-46			
The plot to kill Jesus	26:1-5	14:1-2	22:1-2	
The anointing at Bethany	26:6-13	14:3-9		12:2-8
The plot to kill Lazarus				12:9-11
Judas agrees to betray Jesus	26:14-16	14:10-11	22:3-6	

WEDNESDAY

The Passover supper prepared	26:17-19	14:12-16	22:7-13	
Greeks seek to see Jesus				12:20-26
Jesus predicts his death				12:27-36
Who has believed our report?				12:37-41
Walk in the light				12:42-50

IN THE UPPER ROOM

Jesus eats the Passover	26:20-21	14:17-18	22:14-18	
The disciples argue about greatness			22:24-30	
Jesus washes the disciples feet				13:1-20
Judas goes out	26:21-25	14:18-21	22:21-23	13:21-30
Jesus institutes the Lord's supper	26:26-29	14:22-25	22:19-20	
The new commandment				13:31-35
Jesus predicts Peter's denial			22:31-34	13:36-38
The Way, the Truth and the Life				14:1-6
The Father revealed in the Son				14:7-11
The answered prayer				14:12-14
The Holy Spirit promised				14:15-18
Indwelling of the Father and the Son				14:19-24
The gift of peace				14:25-31
The True Vine				15:1-8

Love and joy perfected				15:9-17
The world's hatred				15:18-27
The coming rejection				16:1-4
The work of the Holy Spirit				16:5-15
Sorrow will be turned to joy				16:16-24
Christ has overcome the world				16:25-33
The glory of the Father and the Son				17:1-5
Jesus prays for his own				17:6-26
Wallet, bag and sword			22:35-38	
Goes out to Gethsemane	26:30	14:26	22:39	18:1
The sheep will be scattered	26:31-35	14:27-31		

THURSDAY

Passover the lamb slain (Ex. 12:6, Lev. 23:5)				
Preparation Day (Jewish tradition)	(27:62)	(15:42)	(23:54)	(19:14)
The prayer in the garden	26:36-46	14:32-42	22:40-46	
Betrayal and arrest	26:47-58	14:43-54	22:47-54	18:2-14
Judged by the high priest	26:59-68	14:55-65	22:66-71	18:19-24 18:15-18
Peter's denial	26:69-75	14:66-72	22:55-62	18:25-27 18:28-40
Judged by Pilate	27:1-26	15:1-15	23:1-25	19:5-16
Judas hangs himself	27:3-10			

The soldiers mock Jesus	27:27-31	15:16-20	(22:63-65)	19:1-4
The King on the cross	27:32-44	15:21-32	23:26-43	19:17-24
Jesus's mother				19:25-27
Jesus lays down his life (John 10:17-18)	27:45-51	15:33-41	23:44-49	19:28-37
Many come out of the graves	27:52-56			
The burial in Joseph's tomb	27:57-61	15:42-47	23:50-56	19:38-42

FRIDAY

Feast of unleavened bread (Lev 23:6-8)				
A high day (Sabbath)	(27:62)	(15:42)	(23:54)	(19:31)
Pilate sets a guard	27:62-66			

SATURDAY

The weekly Sabbath (Lev 23:3)	(28:1)	(16:1)	(23:56)	

SUNDAY

Feast of first fruits (Lev 23:9-14)	28:1	16:2	24:1	20:1
The resurrection (Matt 12:40)	(28:9)	(16:9)	(24:15)	
The women at the empty tomb	28:1-8	16:1-8	24:1-11	20:1-2
Peter and John at the tomb			24:12	20:3-10
Jesus appears to the women	28:9-10	16:9-11		20:11-18
Chief priests bribe the soldiers	28:11-15			
On the road to Emmaus		16:12-13	24:13-35	

Jesus appears in the upper room		16:14	24:36-45	20:19-23

<u>THE SUBSEQUENT 40 DAYS</u> (Acts 1:3)

Jesus appears the second Sunday				20:24-29
John's testimony to Jesus				20:30-31
Jesus at Galilee	28:16-17			21:1-14
Peter restored, 'Follow thou me'				21:15-25
The apostles commissioned	28:18-20	16:15-18	24:46-49	
Jesus taken up into heaven (Acts 1:9)		16:19-20	24:50-53	

TEACHING IN LUKE NOT IN THE CHRONOLOGY

TEACHING IN LUKE NOT IN THE CHRONOLOGY

EVENTS	LUKE
A friend comes at midnight	11:5-8
Keeping the word	11:27-28
The lamp of the body	11:33-36
Beware of Hypocrisy	12:1-3
The fear of God	12:4-7
Confess Christ before men	12:8-12
Parable of the rich fool	12:13-21
Christ brings division	12:49-53
Make peace with your adversary	12:57-59
Repent or perish	13:1-5
Parable of the barren fig tree	13:6-9
A spirit of infirmity	13:10-17
Are there few who are saved?	13:22-30
Jesus must die at Jerusalem	13:31-33
A man with dropsy healed	14:1-6
Take the lowest place	14:7-14
Parable of the great supper	14:15-24
Leaving all to follow Christ	14:25-33
Parable of the lost sheep	14:1-7
Parable of the lost coin	15:8-10
Parable of the lost son	15:11-32

Parable of the unjust steward	16:1-13
The law, the prophets, and the kingdom	16:14-18
The rich man and Lazarus	16:19-31
Jesus warns of offences	17:1-4
Faith and duty	17:5-10
Ten lepers cleansed	17:11-19
The coming of the kingdom	17:20-37
Parable of the persistent widow	18:1-8
Parable of the Pharisee and the tax collector	18:9-14

****

MORE ON CHRONOLOGY

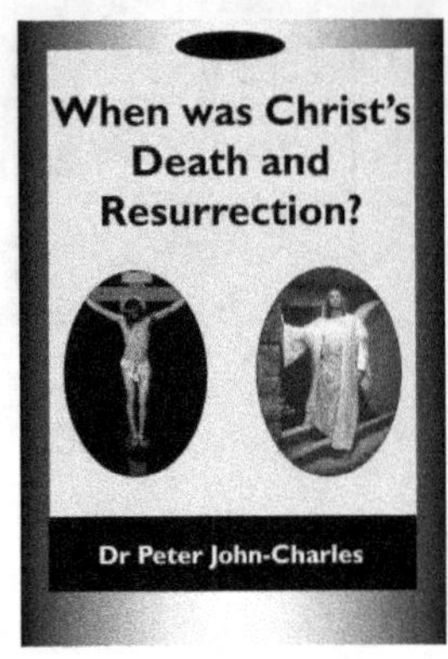

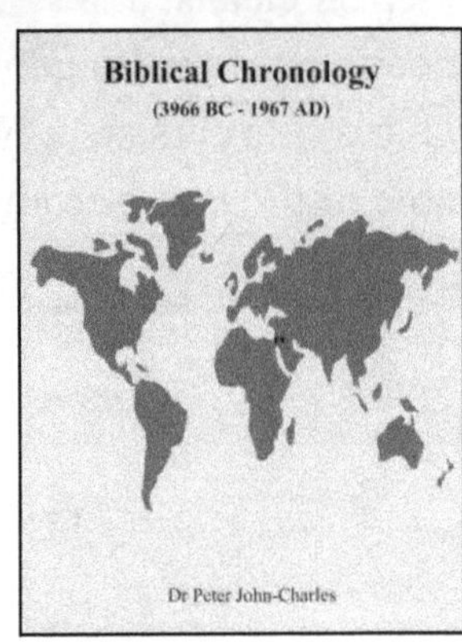

When was Christ's Death and Resurrection?
by Dr. Peter John-Charles
A detailed chronology of the week leading up to Christ's crucifixion and resurrection.

Biblical Chronology (3996 BC – 1967 AD)
by Dr. Peter John-Charles
(Available as an A4 sized perfect bound paperback.)

Further details of these books can be seen on **www.obt.org.uk**

They can be ordered from that website and also from

The Open Bible Trust
Fordland Mount, Upper Basildon,
Reading, RG8 8LU, UK.

MORE ON THE GOSPELS

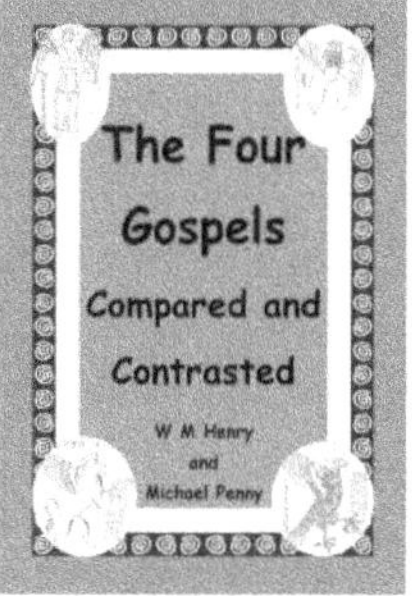

Further details of these books can be seen on **www.obt.org.uk**

They can be ordered from that website and also from

The Open Bible Trust
Fordland Mount, Upper Basildon,
Reading, RG8 8LU, UK.

They are also avaialble as eBooks from Amazon and Apple and as KDP paperbacks from Amazon.

SEARCH MAGAZINE

ABOUT THE AUTHOR

Denis Manley was born in Aldershot, Hampshire, in 1930 and was educated at West End Boys School, mainly during the war years. On leaving school he worked as an improver for the War Department at a power station before becoming an electrical design engineer (installations) with Unigate Ltd. He retired on medical grounds in 1990 and he lived with his wife in Ash, Surrey.

ABOUT THIS BOOK

The Chronology of the Gospel of Jesus Christ

Modern, westernised man likes to know when things happened and the order in which they happened. This was not the case in New Testament times, and it is not the case in many cultures of today's world.

The author has taken Matthew's Gospel as being the one which has events mainly in chronological order and, with the use of many valuable tables, tied what is said in the other three to Matthew. The result gives the student a very good idea of when things happened and the order in which their occurred.

Publications of the Open Bible Trust must be in accordance with its evangelical, fundamental and dispensational basis. However, beyond this minimum, writers are free to express whatever beliefs they may have as their own understanding, provided that the aim in so doing is to further the object of the Open Bible Trust. A copy of the doctrinal basis is available on www.obt.org.uk or from:

THE OPEN BIBLE TRUST
Fordland Mount, Upper Basildon,
Reading, RG8 8LU, GB

www.ingramcontent.com/pod-product-compliance
Lightning Source LLC
LaVergne TN
LVHW010545100826
845148LV00013B/2609

* 9 7 8 1 7 8 3 6 4 5 2 7 5 *